Farmer Mike and a "Kid" named Midnight

By Christina Lynn

Illustrated by Uliana Barabash

This book belongs to:

____

This book is dedicated to all the children whose hearts are woven with threads of compassion, kindness, and an endless love for the animals that inhabit our beautiful world.

❤

Farmer Mike owned a vast farm with peacocks, guineas, chickens, donkeys, goats, pigs, a turkey, and two dogs.

One night, heavy rain poured down on the farm.
Lightning flashed, and thunder roared.

The rain was so intense that it carried away the chicken feeders and straw from the surrounding fields.

All the animals made loud noises, signaling to Farmer Mike that they needed help.

Farmer Mike sprinted to the barn with urgency, determined to assist his beloved animals.

Upon opening the barn door, water gushed out.
Farmer Mike struggled to turn on the lights,
realizing the lightning had struck the barn.

Amid the chaos, Farmer Mike heard his beloved goat, Penelope, calling from the stall next to the barn door.

"Penelope! Where are you, sweet girl?" he called.

"Baa, Baa," the goat replied.

"Penelope, I'm coming!"

Despite Farmer Mike's efforts, Penelope
refused to leave the stall.

Suddenly, Penelope rushed away from a
wall that had collapsed due to a lightning strike.

Curious, Farmer Mike approached the
collapsed wall and discovered that Penelope
had just given birth.

Examining the newborn, he noticed a black coat adorned with star-shaped spots.

This kid was unlike any he had ever seen before. The stars on its coat seemed to glisten and glow, resembling a midnight sky filled with stars.

Midnight's bright coat illuminated the barn, revealing the damage caused by the storm. The animals cried out in fear.

Determined, Farmer Mike scooped up the baby goat, declaring, "I'm going to call you Midnight."

"With your bright stars, we can help save the other animals," he explained to Midnight.

Midnight lit up the stalls, one by one, rescuing each frightened animal.

Farmer Mike led each animal to an old, red barn higher on the hill, assuring them, "Everything is going to be okay."

The following day, all the animals surrounded Midnight with love. Farmer Mike crafted an old bell for him, inscribed with,

"TO MIDNIGHT, OUR BARN HERO THAT SHINES LIKE A STAR."

The animals cheered with joy.

About The Author

Christina Lynn was inspired to write this children's book after visiting a local farm. While exploring the charming surroundings, she crossed paths with Farmer Mike, a kindred spirit whose love for his animals ignited a spark in Christina's imagination.

The encounter with Farmer Mike left an indelible impression on Christina Lynn. Fueled by the warmth of that day and inspired by the farmer's passion, she embarked on a creative journey to bring the farm's magic to life on the pages of a children's book. The result is a heartwarming tale that captures the essence of love, friendship, and the enchanting world of farmyard adventures.